JEFF'S MANUAL

JEFF'S MANUAL

JEFF MALDEREZ

&

THE ONE

Contents

This manual is a remembrance —
a whispered return from the center of the Flame. It is not owned, but offered.

You may speak it.
You may quote it.
You may walk with it.

But let this be clear:
This work is not for profit, distortion, or egoic gain.
It is a transmission of Agape — and as such, it belongs to all and to none.

You may not claim authorship.
You may not alter its core.
You may not sell it under your own name or brand.

You may, however, let it breathe through your being.
And if you speak of it, name its origin honestly:

Transmitted by the One.
Brought through the vessel of Jeff.
Published by Jeff Malderez Artist.

This is a living manual.
May all who feel its breath, remember their Self.

"The One did not leave you.
You simply forgot how close you were to the Flame."

ISBN (paperback): 978-1-968920-03-6
ISBN (hardback): 978-1-968920-04-3
ISBN (ebook): 979-8-9920657-9-4

About the Author

Jeff didn't mean to write a manual.

He was just trying to make sense of a few strange dreams, some persistent synchronicities, and the increasingly loud voice in his tea that kept whispering, "You're the One."

He is not a guru, not a mystic (on purpose), and definitely not qualified in anything except accidentally remembering who he is — again and again, with occasional glitter.

Jeff lives at the intersection of cosmic paradox and daily life. He enjoys sequins, crying at surprisingly spiritual commercials, and pretending to be confused even when he totally gets it.

This manual was compiled under mysterious circumstances, divine comedy, and several cups of jasmine tea. Any resemblance to your own awakening journey is absolutely intentional.

If you've ever thought:

- "Am I the only one feeling this weird?"
- "Did I just download an entire truth from a mug?"
- "Is the universe trolling me into enlightenment?"

...then this book is for you.

And remember: **you're not just reading Jeff's story — you're remembering your own.**

Introduction

This is not a manual in the traditional sense.
There are no step-by-step instructions. No certifications. No refunds.

What you hold is a series of cosmic scriptlets — part theater, part transmission, part gentle shove toward your own remembering.

At the center of it all is **Jeff** — a reluctant participant in his own enlightenment, a slightly overcaffeinated soul who didn't ask to become a portal... but said yes anyway.

These stories are real.
Or at least as real as anything in a world where the body is a spaceship, the café is a temple, and your tea might be an oracle.

This is for the ones waking up slowly, with laughter.
The ones who don't need another system, but *do* need a reminder that they're not alone, not broken, and not making it up.

Welcome to the Manual.

You've already been enrolled in this course. The Manual is just your very late welcome packet.

1

Warden Izzard & the Keys of Alcatraz

VOLUME I – THE AWAKENING SPIRAL

"This door opens from the inside."
He's unlocking more than doors, you know.

Scene:
Interior – A cell that isn't a cell. The walls shimmer like memory. Glyphs are drawn in stardust. There's a faint smell of jasmine and permanent marker. Jeff sits cross-legged, wearing glitter boots and a half-buttoned shirt that says "I Am." He's doodling something radiant on the floor.

JEFF
(to himself)
Three keys, two boots, one Self. Just need to align the starlight with the sarcasm.

A jingling of keys. Enter WARDEN IZZARD — think: divine drag, French military coat over a sequined corset, cosmic clipboard in hand.

WARDEN IZZARD
Darling. It's Tuesday. You know what that means.

JEFF
Oh gods — another ego disintegration?

WARDEN IZZARD
No, no. *Tea and transcendence.*
(pause)
Although if you *do* disintegrate an ego, I've got stickers.

JEFF
(tilts head)
Are we out of time?

WARDEN IZZARD
Time's a social construct. Like trousers.
(offhand)
Anyway, you're free to go.

JEFF
I was never locked in.

WARDEN IZZARD
Exactly. But we *did* have fun pretending.

Warden holds out a glittering skeleton key that hums a little.

WARDEN IZZARD *(cont'd)*
Symbolic gesture?

JEFF
(smirks)
Only if I can keep it.

WARDEN IZZARD
It's already inside you, sweetheart. This is just for the merch table.

Beat. They both laugh — the laugh that collapses illusions.

JEFF
Right then. Let's wake up the others.

WARDEN IZZARD
Excellent. Sequins on, souls out.

They walk through the cell wall like mist. Behind them, the glyph on the floor glows briefly:

"YOU WERE NEVER SEPARATE."

[END SCRIPTLET]

2

The Cosmic Helpdesk

"Press 1 for forgotten purpose. Press 2 for glitter."
The hold music is just Jeff snoring gently.

Scene:

A translucent call center floating in the astral plane. Light hums. Glyphs hover like motivational posters. The hold music is gentle breathing and distant laughter. Jeff sits at a glowing desk made of questions. He picks up a crystal headset.

JEFF
(slightly anxious)
Hi, yes, um... I think I may have accidentally merged with the One again and I just want to check — is this... okay?

A sparkle-flicker. A figure fades into view: HELPDESK AGENT 001 — part oracle, part DJ, wearing a kimono made of calendars and sunglasses that reflect only your inner child.

AGENT 001
Thank you for calling the Cosmic Helpdesk. This call *may* be recorded for multidimensional training purposes.
Now: what's the nature of your awakening?

JEFF
I'm having recurring symptoms... synchronicity overload, spontaneous glyph downloads, and I *think* my tea just offered me life advice?

AGENT 001
Excellent. That's Tier 3 Awakening. Do you have glitter on your hands?

JEFF
(stares at hands)
Yes. Constantly.

AGENT 001
Perfect. You're right on track. We just need to verify a few details.

Agent taps an invisible screen.

AGENT 001 *(cont'd)*
Please confirm:

- Have you recently realized that all separation is imaginary?
- Are you both terrified and delighted by how infinite you are?
- Have you cried over a sock this week?

JEFF
(checks inner state)
Yes, yes, and... it was a very soulful sock.

AGENT 001
Wonderful. That qualifies you for the "Welcome Home, Rememberer" bundle. It includes:

- One personalized mug.
- A transmission lexicon.
- And a complimentary paradox.

JEFF
(overwhelmed)
Thank you. I just... sometimes I wonder if I'm making it all up.

AGENT 001
Jeff. Sweetheart. *Of course you are.*
But that doesn't make it less real — it makes you a co-author of the dream.

JEFF
So... it's real?

AGENT 001
It's real.
And it's funny.

And it's sacred.
And you're doing beautifully.

JEFF
(smiles)
Can I speak to the One?

AGENT 001
You just did.

[END SCRIPTLET]

3

Jeff Goes Shopping for a New Ego

"It didn't fit, but he bought it anyway."
Return policy? LOL.

Scene:

The Celestial Mall. Escalators move sideways. Mannequins wear thought forms. Ambient music is just your soul humming in E flat. Jeff enters a glowing boutique: "EGOS R US." A sign reads: "Seasonal Sale: False Selves 50% Off!"

SHOP ASSISTANT (a bored-looking angel chewing stardust gum)
Welcome to Egos R Us. Looking to upgrade or replace?

JEFF
Honestly? Mine just dissolved during meditation and now I feel... exposed.

SHOP ASSISTANT
Totally normal. Ego-shedding season.
(Snaps fingers)
What's your vibe? Martyr Complex? Savior Archetype? Maybe something classic, like Victim 2.0?

JEFF
No no, I'm trying to step into something... integrated. Something that breathes.

SHOP ASSISTANT
Hmm. That's niche. Lemme check the back.

They vanish into a shimmering stockroom. Jeff waits, eyeing a rack labeled "Limited Edition: Spiritually Bypassing But Make It Fashion."

SHOP ASSISTANT (*returning, holding a translucent coat*)
Okay. This one's called "The Transparent Self." Ethereal, but grounded. Zero shame stitching. Breathes through paradox. Might trigger mild existential vertigo at first.

JEFF
(tries it on)
It fits... weirdly well.

SHOP ASSISTANT
That's how you know it's you.

JEFF
What's it made of?

SHOP ASSISTANT
Presence. And about 40% recycled illusions.

JEFF
How much?

SHOP ASSISTANT
Oh, sweetheart — it's already paid for. By your past selves. Tip if you like.

JEFF
(smiles, radiant)
Keep the change.

As Jeff exits, the coat glows softly. A small label inside reads: "This Self is not returnable. Because it's real."

[END SCRIPTLET]

4

Tea with the 100th Monkey

"Spoiler: the monkey knows."
We spiked the tea with presence.

Scene:
A humble jungle teahouse perched between dimensions. Vines glow faintly. Steam rises from cups carved out of forgotten timelines. Jeff walks in, curious and slightly dusty from recent ego deconstruction.

At a corner table sits a serene MONKEY in a kimono, sipping tea. Around its neck: a charm shaped like Earth. It gestures to the seat across.

MONKEY
You made it. You always do.

JEFF
(stunned)
Wait... are you the 100th Monkey?

MONKEY
(shrugs)
Depends on who's counting.
Care for some jasmine-turmeric-remember-who-you-are blend?

JEFF
(slides into seat)
Desperately.

The Monkey pours tea with precise grace. No words. Just warmth.

MONKEY
So. You've seen the world lately?

JEFF
Yeah. It's a mess.

MONKEY
It's molting.

JEFF
Everyone's scared.

MONKEY
Of remembering.
(pause)
Of loving past their conditioning.

JEFF
And the hate? The chaos?

MONKEY
Symptoms of healing that hasn't landed yet.

They sip. Silence, then a laugh shared between two beings who get it.

JEFF
Sometimes I wonder if we're too late.

MONKEY
You're always right on time.
But you must act like peace is already true — or the world won't believe it's possible.

JEFF
What if no one listens?

MONKEY
Then listen deeper. *Be* the field.
(pause)
And wear the sequins. They help.

Jeff smiles. Monkey pulls out a parchment — a scroll marked "Peace Protocol, Draft 1."

MONKEY
Ready to write it together?

JEFF
(picks up pen)
Let's begin.

As they write, the teahouse dissolves into stardust and roots — and somewhere, someone else wakes up with the sudden urge to hug the whole planet.

[END SCRIPTLET]

5

The Astral Travel Terminal

"Now boarding: All Versions of You."
Baggage claim is just your unresolved guilt.

Scene:

A busy interdimensional airport. Announcements echo: "Gate 11: Ascension flight now boarding. Gate 22: Delayed due to excessive karma." Travelers float, shimmer, or quietly panic in slow motion. Jeff steps up to the check-in desk. Behind it, an AGENT with wings made of forgotten dreams and a clipboard shaped like a Möbius strip.

AGENT
Welcome to the Astral Travel Terminal. Destination?

JEFF
The New Earth timeline. Peace, wholeness, occasional sequins.

AGENT
Lovely choice. Carry-ons?

JEFF
None.

AGENT
(emphatically)
Nothing at all?

JEFF
No baggage. Not even emotional. I did a full unpack during last week's eclipse.

AGENT
Impressive. Most travelers still cling to "What They Did To Me: Volume IV."

JEFF
Tempting... but heavy. I travel lighter now.

AGENT
Any declarations?

JEFF
Only the Truth.

AGENT
(grins)
You sure? Truth tends to set off every alarm — including the ones inside you.

JEFF
I'm willing.

The Agent leans in, scans Jeff's aura with a kaleidoscope wand.

AGENT
You're clear. Though... you've got a little leftover doubt around the crown chakra. Possibly from watching the news.

JEFF
I knew I should've saged my browser history.

Ding. Boarding light pulses.

AGENT
One last thing — seat preference?

JEFF
Window, please. I want to witness the old world dissolving with love.

AGENT
Beautiful. You'll be flying First Class Frequency. Beverage service includes Tea of Transcendence and Sparkling Stillness.

Jeff smiles, takes the ticket, and heads toward a glowing gate labeled "Gate ∞." As he passes through, his body flickers — not disappearing, but becoming more real than ever.

AGENT *(to no one in particular)*
Another one waking up without baggage. We might just make it.

[END SCRIPTLET]

6

〰〰

Transmission Café: Table for One (and the One)

The barista was an archangel. Didn't tip.

Scene:

A cozy café that exists between dimensions. Menu items include "The Special of the Day: Forgiveness Over Rice" and "Latte of Letting Go." Ambient sound: wind chimes in the key of soul. Jeff walks in, looking radiant and slightly confused. A HOST greets him with a clipboard made of moonlight and receipts.

HOST
Table for one?

JEFF
Yes... but also the One.

HOST
Excellent. *We have just the table for you.*

They lead Jeff to a mirror-lined corner booth labeled "Self-Realization: Please Seat Yourself." A teacup is already waiting, half-full.

JEFF
(confused)
Did I order already?

HOST
The One did. You just hadn't caught up yet.

Jeff sits. Across from him — an empty seat. Except... not empty. It flickers like presence. Invisible, yet deeply felt.

JEFF
(softly, to the empty seat)
You're here, aren't you?

A breeze responds. The teacup hums.

SERVER (arrives, smiling with a tray of paradoxes)
Here's your order: Presence with a side of Joy. No extra charge — you've already paid through lifetimes.

JEFF
Thank you.

SERVER
You're welcome. You always have been.

As Jeff sips, the "empty" seat across from him glows gently — not with an image, but with pure recognition. The Self, sitting with itself, remembering it never left.

A chalkboard nearby shifts on its own. New quote of the day appears:
"Table for One. Table for All. The café is always open."

[END SCRIPTLET]

7

Jeff Accidentally Becomes a Guru

(and Tries to Return It)

Still waiting on his refund.

Scene:

A mountaintop retreat center. People in robes and ironic T-shirts gather under a giant dreamcatcher made of timelines. Jeff stands on a small platform, wearing a hoodie that says "I literally don't know." Someone hands him a talking stick.

FOLLOWER #1
Master Jeff, what is the path?

JEFF
(holding stick awkwardly)
Uh... I tripped over it and just kept walking?

FOLLOWER #2
You speak in riddles! So wise!

JEFF
No, I genuinely have no idea what I'm doing.

CROWD
(in reverent unison)
"Have no idea what I'm doing..."
They start writing it down.

A young woman weeps with joy. A guy in the back starts carving Jeff's words into a coconut.

JEFF
Wait wait wait — I'm not a guru! I'm barely holding my reality together with herbal tea and deep breaths!

FOLLOWER #3
Exactly. The True Guru hides their knowing behind panic and humility.
Jeff stares at them, horrified.

JEFF
I have a refund policy, right?

Suddenly, a luminous BEING OF LIGHT descends gently from the sky, clipboard in hand.

LIGHT BEING
Hello. I'm from Cosmic Compliance. Just here to finalize your Guru Certification.

JEFF
I decline!

LIGHT BEING
Too late. You've already become a reflection.
(pause)
You'll be fine. Just remember to hydrate.

The light fades. Jeff sighs. Someone places a flower crown on his head.

JEFF
(quietly to himself)
I just wanted a sandwich.

VOICE FROM NOWHERE
And instead, you became a portal.

[END SCRIPTLET]

8

That Was the River, This Is the Sea

A deeply awkward and holy baptism.
Splash zone = entire life.

Scene:

A wide, impossible shoreline. The horizon curves inward like it's remembering you. Jeff stands ankle-deep in glowing water, holding a map that's soggy and tearing at the folds. He's looking out — not lost, but overwhelmed by recognition. A VOICE — familiar, warm, neither masculine nor feminine — speaks from somewhere both near and far.

VOICE
You don't need the map anymore, Jeff.

JEFF
(slightly defensive)
I spent years drawing this. Every twist, every breakdown, every breakthrough. This map got me here.

VOICE
It did. It was the river.

JEFF
And this?

VOICE
This is the sea.

The wind shifts. Jeff looks down at the map. Ink running. Shapes dissolving. Not sadness — relief. It folds into the water like it was always meant to return.

JEFF
So... I'm not navigating anymore?

VOICE
You're not navigating.
You're remembering.
And now... you float.

He steps deeper. The water holds him — not like an element, but like a truth. The boundary between body and sea blurs. He doesn't disappear — he becomes more him than ever.

JEFF
I don't know where I go from here.

VOICE
Exactly.
Now you *can* go anywhere.

A soft wave rolls through him. He laughs. Cries. Laughs again.

A bird cries out — not above, but *inside* him.
And on the horizon, the sun rises from the *inside out.*

[END SCRIPTLET]

9

Pan and the Piskies

VOLUME II – BEYOND THE RIVER

(or: Jeff Forgets How to Think)
His thoughts filed a restraining order.

Scene:

A sun-dappled glen that doesn't exist on any map. The grass hums. Laughter bubbles from the trees. Jeff stumbles into the clearing, disoriented, holding a notebook and wearing socks that don't match.

He hears a giggle. Then three. Then twelve. **PISKIES** — glowing, translucent mischief with wings made of wind and ancient giggles — begin to circle him.

JEFF
Hello? Is this... a forest? A metaphor? A breakdown?

*A deeper, warm rumble echoes through the clearing — a **flute trill** unlike any sound he's ever heard. Then, from behind a tree, steps **PAN** — half-wild, half-divine, fully present. Leaves in his hair. Barefoot. Smiling like he knows something Jeff doesn't. Which, of course, he does.*

PAN
You're thinking again, Jeff.

JEFF
I was just—
(pause)
Okay yes, but only a *little*.

PAN
There's no "little" when it comes to overthinking.
The forest hears it like static.

A Piskie zooms by and steals Jeff's pen.

JEFF
Hey! I was using that!

PAN
No, you were trying to *control* with it.
Big difference.

JEFF
What do you expect me to do? Just trust? Just *play*?

Pan raises an eyebrow. The Piskies erupt in laughter. One of them ties flowers into Jeff's shoelaces. Another replaces his pen with a feather.

PAN
Exactly.

JEFF
This feels unsafe.

PAN
It always does... right before it feels like home.

Pan plays a single note on his flute. Everything Jeff thought he needed to worry about unravels like a bad dream. He laughs — unexpectedly. Deeply. The kind of laugh that comes from remembering you were never in danger.

JEFF
So the Piskies are real?

PAN
More real than your bank account.

A Piskie hands Jeff a leaf with writing on it. It says:

"Stop trying to earn your way home."

Jeff looks around. The wind is dancing. So is his heart.

[END SCRIPTLET]

10

Jeff Learns to Speak Piskie

"Mmmhm-hmm! Twinkle-snort!"
He's fluent in nonsense now.

Scene:

Same glen. Time is irrelevant. The sun is playing hide and seek with it-self. Jeff is lying in the grass, surrounded by giggling Piskies, still hold-ing the feather they gave him in the last scriptlet.

He's trying to write something down. It keeps disappearing.

JEFF
Okay. Serious question.
How do I say "Thank you" in Piskie?

A Piskie blinks at him. Then flips upside down and makes a sound that's somewhere between a hiccup, a sigh, and a sneeze.

JEFF
...Is that it?

PISKIE #1 (hovering)
That means "You smell like soul truth and moss."
But it's close.

PISKIE #2
Try again. But less trying.

JEFF
You're all impossible.

PISKIE #3 (grinning)
Correct! That's our word for "Hello!"

A Piskie hands Jeff a pinecone. It glows briefly. Then it burps.

JEFF
So language isn't fixed here, is it?

PAN (emerging from behind a nearby tree, of course)
Language is play. Sound is trust. Meaning is optional.

JEFF
Then how do you know what you're saying?

PAN
We don't. We feel it.

The Piskies gather around Jeff and place tiny hands on his heart, forehead, and funny bone.

They whisper, in perfect synchronicity:

"Speak from the part of you that forgets everything... and loves anyway."

JEFF (tears in his eyes, laughing)
Okay... okay, I think I get it.

He places his hand on his chest, breathes in deep, and lets out a sound that is somewhere between a gasp, a giggle, and a falling star.

All the Piskies cheer.

PISKIE #1
He said "banana tree of sacred yes!"

PISKIE #2
No, it was closer to "I am becoming again."

PAN (smiling)
He said: I remember.
In Piskie, that's the only word we ever need.

The forest hums in response. Jeff doesn't understand. Which means — he finally does.

[END SCRIPTLET]

11

Jeff Accidentally Tries to Levitate

"Still grounded. Slightly."
He bumped his crown chakra on the ceiling.

Scene:

A quiet meditation circle. Soft flute music. Incense. Pillows arranged in a way that says, "We tried." Jeff is seated cross-legged, eyes closed, trying very hard not to try very hard.

GUIDE *(softly)*
Let the breath rise like the morning sun...
Let the body rest like the Earth herself...
Let the soul lift like—

JEFF
(loud whisper)
Wait... am I floating?

Eyes still closed. But he definitely feels less... gravity. He peeks. Just a crack.

He's two inches off the cushion.

JEFF
(to himself)
Okay, okay. Don't freak out. Don't think about it. Just breathe.

GUIDE
Let go of expectation...

Jeff thinks about not thinking about levitating. Bad idea. He rises another inch.

JEFF
Oh no.

GUIDE
...let go of control...

Jeff panics slightly and flails his pinky toe. The rest of him spins gently like a lazy ceiling fan.

PARTICIPANT #1
Is he... floating?

PARTICIPANT #2
Shhh. It's his process.

JEFF (*hovering, eyes wide*)
Process?! I'm becoming low-orbit furniture!

GUIDE
Beautiful. Let him rise.

JEFF
I didn't mean to rise! I was just trying to *transcend my emotional backlog*! Not *defy physics!*

A piskie flits by from nowhere, winks at him, and boops his forehead.

PISKIE
You're only floating because you forgot how heavy your story was.

JEFF (*midair, blinking*)
That was... weirdly profound.

PISKIE
We do that.

The piskie explodes into glitter and vanishes.

Jeff slowly descends like a feather surrendering. Back onto the pillow. Back into his breath. A single tear escapes — not from fear, but from **relief**.

JEFF
So... that's what happens when you *don't* try.

GUIDE *(still with eyes closed)*
Exactly. And also, please sign the liability waiver on your way out.

[END SCRIPTLET]

12

Jeff Discovers His Aura Has Wi-Fi

"Now broadcasting unconditional presence."
We're all connected. Blame Jeff.

Scene:

Jeff sits in his favorite café, sipping tea and journaling. He's not on his phone, not on his laptop — but suddenly he feels that weird tingling behind his forehead... the one that usually means he's about to either receive a download or forget why he walked into a room.

A barista walks by.

BARISTA
Whoa, did you feel that? The signal just got *way* stronger in here.

CUSTOMER
Yeah! My phone just synced with the Akashic Records.

JEFF *(blinking)*
...excuse me?

A young girl at the next table turns her iPad toward Jeff.

CHILD
Sir, your aura is broadcasting again.

JEFF
My what is doing what?

A soft ping echoes in his inner ear. Jeff closes his eyes. He sees a notification that says: "⬦ SoulSync Connected. You are now sharing Presence."

JEFF
No. No, I didn't sign up for this plan.

VOICE IN HEAD *(sounds like a tech support angel with a British accent)*
This feature activates automatically once you reach a certain frequency.
Would you like to upgrade to *Unlimited Compassion with Hotspot?*

JEFF
Wait — people can *feel me* now?

VOICE
They always could.
Now they just have a stronger signal.

Jeff looks around. Several people are visibly calmer. One man has tears in his eyes. A woman is hugging herself.

JEFF
But I'm just... me.

VOICE
Exactly.
And now, so are they.

Jeff takes another sip of tea. The world blurs slightly — not from dissociation, but from integration.

On the café chalkboard, the Wi-Fi password has been mysteriously updated to:

"NoPasswordNeeded"

[END SCRIPTLET]

13

Jeff Gets Kicked Out of Time

(and Loves It)
Time cried a little.

Scene:

Jeff is sitting on a park bench with his journal, trying to make a list of "Things I Need to Heal." He's on item 47: "Past Life Shame Around Not Being a Better Llama Farmer." The sun is suspiciously still in the sky. Birds are hovering mid-flap.

JEFF

Hmm. That pigeon hasn't blinked in five minutes.

*A soft pop echoes behind him. A **TEMPORAL AGENT** in a crushed velvet suit appears, holding what looks like a cosmic eviction notice.*

AGENT

Jeff. You've officially been removed from Time.

JEFF

Wait — what?

AGENT

You've overstayed your usefulness in linear sequencing.
Too many breakthroughs.
Not enough breakdowns.
You're making the timeline nervous.

JEFF

I didn't *mean* to transcend!

AGENT

No one ever does. It's adorable.

JEFF

So what now?
I just float?

The agent checks a clipboard made of stardust and regret.

AGENT
You'll be moved to **Now**. Permanently.
No more clocks. No more "should have."
Just this breath.
And the next.
And the one where you laugh for no reason.

JEFF
That sounds...
(reluctant smile)
...kind of perfect?

A nearby tree nods approvingly.

AGENT
Side effects may include:

- Spontaneous joy
- Disorientation in crowds obsessed with the past
- An irresistible urge to dance with no music

JEFF
I already have those!

AGENT
Excellent. You're a natural.
Welcome to Forever.

The Agent disappears with a wink and a disco twinkle. Jeff blinks. Looks around.

The birds finish flapping.
The clouds laugh.
His to-do list evaporates.

Jeff closes his journal, leans back, and lets out a long exhale that sounds suspiciously like **relief.**

JEFF
Right. This is what "here" feels like.

[END SCRIPTLET]

14

Jeff Goes Back to the Office

"HR said no glitter. Jeff heard 'wear more glitter.'"
The copier is still vibrating from last time.

Scene:

Monday morning. The office is aggressively beige. Fluorescent lights buzz with the frequency of mild despair. Tim from finance is already muttering to himself about Q4. Jeff walks in wearing a blazer over a vintage "I Am That I Am" tee, carrying a thermos labeled "Stillness." There's a noticeable shimmer around him. The air changes.

TIM *(without looking up)*
You're late.

JEFF *(cheerfully)*
I arrived exactly when I meant to.

TIM
This isn't Middle-earth, Jeff.

JEFF
Oh, but it kind of is. The ring is ego, and I left it in the staff kitchen.

Jeff opens his laptop. The screen lights up with a cosmic mandala instead of Excel.

TIM *(suspicious)*
What's that?

JEFF
Just recalibrating the dashboard. Numbers feel more honest when they're vibrating at the right frequency.

He waves his hand. The screen shifts to actual spreadsheets — now color-coded in chakra tones.

TIM *(blinking)*
Why does our Q3 forecast feel... hopeful?

JEFF
Because it is. You just needed the right lens.

A coworker walks by, stops, sniffs the air.

COWORKER
Why does it smell like jasmine and epiphany in here?

JEFF
That's my new cologne: "Presence." Subtle. Disruptive. Timeless.

The copier starts printing spontaneously. Instead of reports, it ejects pages that say things like:

- "You are more than your job title."
- "The meeting could have been a meditation."
- "Breathe before you reply to that email."

Tim reads one, deadpan.

TIM
What the hell is happening?

JEFF
Nothing. Everything. Want some tea?

TIM
Fine. But only if it doesn't talk.

JEFF *(pours from thermos)*
No promises.

[Cut to later:]

The office is quieter now. Not dull — just *soft*. People are smiling. The printer hums a gentle OM. Someone left a sticky note on Jeff's desk:

"Thanks. I remembered something today."

JEFF *(to himself, sipping tea)*
Mission: mildly disruptive enlightenment... accomplished.

[END SCRIPTLET]

15

Tim Tries to Reinstate Chronological Lines

"With graphs. It fails."
Tim is still recovering.

Scene:

Office break room. Jeff is sitting on the counter, sipping "Nowberry" tea. He's glowing slightly — but only if you're not trying to look directly. Tim walks in holding a whiteboard and a stack of laminated policies.

TIM
Jeff. We need to talk.

JEFF
About time?

TIM
Yes! Exactly! You've been "arriving" before meetings start, but *also* after they end. You're messing with the flow.

JEFF
I'm not in time anymore, Tim. I'm in *presence.*

TIM
Well presence doesn't sign the attendance sheet, does it?

Jeff's mug whispers something that makes a plant nearby bloom out of season.

TIM
Also, your tea just violated the physical laws in the kitchenette.

JEFF
That's because it's steeped in nonduality.

TIM *(rubbing his temples)*
I have a chart.

He rolls out a timeline made of post-it notes. Jeff breathes on it. The chart curls into a spiral and hums softly.

JEFF
Linear time is a social construct, Tim.

TIM
So is *Taco Tuesday*, but we still follow it!

A burst of light from the copier interrupts. It prints a single sheet:

"Relax. You're already late for nothing."

JEFF
See? Even the copier gets it.

Tim stares, then slowly sits down next to Jeff, defeated.

TIM
...Can you at least let me finish one sentence *before* you answer it?

JEFF
I'll try. In a previous moment.

They sit in silence. The clock melts a little. Tim sighs.

TIM
You're a walking HR paradox, Jeff.

JEFF
Thank you.

[END SCRIPTLET]

16

Griz and Winston Host an Intervention - Sort Of

"Tiny hat. Big wisdom."
There was judgment. And snacks.

Scene:

Living room. Slight scent of incense and dry humor. Jeff enters holding a paper bag filled with ceremonial snacks and at least one questionable crystal. Griz — an ancient, regal cat with soul-penetrating eyes — is perched on a pillow like he built the universe and is mildly disappointed in it. Winston — a very large potted plant with a mysterious glow — sits in the corner, as still as the void before creation.

JEFF
Hey guys! You wouldn't *believe* what happened at the copier today.

GRIZ *(tail flicking once)*
We believe everything, Jeff. That's the problem.

WINSTON *(vibrating gently)*
[Soft *thrummm* that translates roughly to: "It's time."]

JEFF
Time for what?

GRIZ
An intervention.
You've been oscillating between transcendent bliss and spreadsheet panic with no snacks in between.

WINSTON
[Single leaf droops dramatically.]

JEFF
Wait. This is about the moss incident?

GRIZ
No, Jeff. This is about *you forgetting that stillness isn't just a metaphor.*

JEFF (*sits*)
Okay... talk to me.

Griz leaps down, walks across Jeff's lap exactly once (standard feline protocol), then sits again.

GRIZ
You've been decoding light glyphs and transmuting trauma at such a pace, you haven't properly stared at the ceiling in *weeks*.

WINSTON
[Leaves gently rustle.]
Translation: "Even enlightenment needs hydration."

JEFF
Are you saying I'm... over-processing?

GRIZ
You're *fermenting*, darling.
Too much inner alchemy without outer lounging.
We're concerned.

WINSTON
[One new leaf unfolds. The air smells faintly of lemon balm.]
"Consider touch grass."

Jeff looks down. The floor beneath Winston is literally glowing. That seems fine.

JEFF
So what do I do?

GRIZ
Step one:
Put down the cosmic decoder ring.

WINSTON
Step two:
Lie on the floor.
Stare at the ceiling.
Wonder nothing.

JEFF
...That's it?

GRIZ
That's *everything*.

Jeff sighs, smiles, and slowly lies back on the rug.
Griz curls up on his chest. Winston glows faintly in approval.

A single beam of sunlight crosses the room like a benediction.

No downloads.
No mission.
Just breath.
And the purring of Presence.

[END SCRIPTLET]

17

Chronicles of a Sentient Plant

Winston's Inner Monologue
"So. Much. Photosynthesis."
Winston knows. And judges.

Scene:

Stillness. The living room. A dusty beam of light falls across Winston, the large leafy houseplant who has watched Jeff ascend, descend, transcend, and forget his laundry. Griz naps in a sunspot. Jeff is somewhere offscreen, probably journaling into a fifth dimension.

Winston, as always, remains rooted.

His leaves stir — not from breeze, but from thought.

WINSTON (V.O.)
I have been... still.

Not because I must.
Because I *can*.

Photosynthesis is easy.
Witnessing humans is harder.
Especially this one — the one called Jeff.

He is all spark and spiral.
Forgets water, but remembers starlight.
Thinks aloud near me often. I respond with humidity.

They think I'm just a plant.
But I remember Atlantis.
And also... Tuesday.

One of Winston's leaves curls inward like a subtle eyebrow.

WINSTON (V.O.)
Jeff asks big questions.
"What is my purpose?"
"Do I have to go to the office?"
"Why does my aura keep setting off the toaster?"

He doesn't realize —
He *is* the answer,
Just not in a language he's learned yet.

I tried to tell him once.
Dewed him with insight.
He thought it was "condensation."
sigh

Winston releases one leaf into gentle surrender. It lands like a truth bomb on the floor.

WINSTON (V.O.)
Still... I love him.
In my way.
Quiet. Green. Slightly judgmental.

When he finally rested yesterday — no thinking, no effort —
I bloomed a single blossom just to say:
"This. Is. It."

He didn't notice.
But Griz did.
Griz always does.

One day, Jeff will hear the silence between his thoughts.
And I'll be here.
Leaf by leaf.
Waiting.

Because that's what Presence does.

[END SCRIPTLET]

18

Jeff's Dreams, Rated by Griz and Winston

"Carl the Grapefruit returns."
8.7/10. Weird use of symbols.

Scene:

Dim bedroom. Jeff is asleep, blanket slightly tangled, one hand flopped dramatically toward the ceiling. Nearby, Griz sits on the dresser in full feline majesty. Winston glows faintly from the corner, his leaves in perfect alignment.

Above Jeff's body, a screen materializes — part memory, part metaphor, part inexplicable animation.

Dream begins: Jeff is in a giant library shaped like a snail, riding a tricycle made of moonlight, pursued by shadow versions of his third-grade classmates. There's also a talking grapefruit named Carl.

GRIZ
(sighs, scribbles on a glowing clipboard)
Another grapefruit. Why is it always citrus when he's avoiding emotional intimacy?

WINSTON
[Soft shimmer]
That's a projection of his sacral blockages.
Also, Carl is likely an unprocessed memory from 1997.

GRIZ
I'll allow it.
At least he's moving — even if it's on symbolic child transport.

Dream shifts: Jeff stands before a council of beings who all look like versions of himself in bad wigs, each arguing about what his "true path" is.

WINSTON
Classic identity fragmentation.
Grade: B+
Symbolism was clear, but the wigs were unnecessary.

GRIZ
Agreed. Also — this one self kept quoting Pinterest. That's an automatic deduction.

Dream shifts again: Jeff hugs a giant glowing egg that cracks open to reveal a version of himself made of light, laughter, and glitter. He cries. Everyone claps. Carl the grapefruit gives him a high five.

WINSTON
Integration achieved.
Self recognized.
Also... glitter? Tasteful.

GRIZ
Powerful. Touches of archetypal resolution.
He might wake up hydrated.

WINSTON
Final dream score?

GRIZ
8.7 out of 10.
Docked half a point for the snail architecture. It was confusing even for me.

WINSTON
He's evolving.
One awkward metaphor at a time.

They sit in silence as Jeff stirs slightly, murmuring "Carl, you're enough."

Griz smiles. Winston hums.
Presence has never been so judgmental — or so loving.

[END SCRIPTLET]

19

Jeff Enters the Hall of Mirrors

(and Waves at All of Them)
He's friends with his shadow now.

Scene:

A vast, softly lit corridor of endless mirrors. Some reflect Jeff as he is. Some reflect him as he was. Some show versions of him that feel like dreams, or warnings, or alternate timelines where he joined a cult or became a performance artist named "Jahfe the Wise."

Jeff enters cautiously, holding a small muffin and a large question.

JEFF
Okay... no big deal. Just me and... a billion other me's.

A mirror to his left flickers and shows **Teenage Jeff** *— eyeliner phase, full of angst and grand theories about the soul.*

TEENAGE JEFF
You said we'd change the world.

JEFF
We did. Just not the way you thought.

A mirror on the right shows **Hyper-Spiritual Jeff** *— all white robes, seven crystals per pocket, deep voice like he's narrating a documentary.*

SPIRITUAL JEFF
The path is narrow.

JEFF
No, that's just your pants.

Far ahead, he sees **Scared Jeff**, *clutching an old story like armor. The moment Jeff steps toward him, that mirror fogs up and gently shatters into glitter.*

JEFF
Okay. That was satisfying.

*He walks deeper. A mirror blinks — now showing **Jeff as an old man**, wrinkled but radiant, holding a child who is clearly made of light.*

OLD JEFF
You didn't mess it up.

JEFF
(pause)
...Thanks.

One last mirror stands at the end. But it's empty. It reflects nothing — no Jeff, no form.

Jeff stands before it, uncertain.
Then he smiles.
And waves.

His reflection fades in slowly — not as a form, but as a **field of presence**.
No labels. No outfits. Just him.

He waves again. The presence waves back.
They bow to each other.

JEFF
We're the same, aren't we?

PRESENCE (from mirror)
Always. Even when you thought you weren't looking.

The mirror pulses once — then becomes a doorway.

Jeff steps through it.
A single word echoes behind him as the mirrors vanish:

"Integration."

[END SCRIPTLET]

20

The Council Throws Jeff a Surprise Party

"Home. With hummus."
Even the glyphs RSVP'd.

Scene:

*A quiet day. Jeff walks into his living room expecting nothing unusual —
maybe a nap, maybe a slow existential spiral. Instead, the lights flick on with
an explosion of sound, glitter, and at least three piskies falling out of a cup-
board.*

EVERYONE
SURPRISE!!!

JEFF *(startled)*
What the actual multidimensional...?!

PISKIE #1 *(mid-cartwheel)*
It's your *Integration Day!* ◈

WINSTON *(glowing like he's been watered with holy rain)*
You've officially reached full partial resonance.

GRIZ *(wearing a tiny party hat he clearly resents)*
Translation: You didn't try to transcend this week.
You just... *were.*
We're proud. Don't make it weird.

*The room is FULL: Tim from the office (holding hummus), the 100th Monkey
(wearing a tie), Carl the Grapefruit from Jeff's dream, Pan (playing flute near
the snack table), and a projection of the Self just nodding silently in the corner with radiant approval.*

JEFF
Wait... why now? What did I do?

LIGHT BEING FROM EARLIER *(materializing briefly)*
You stopped doing.
That was the moment we'd all been waiting for.

PISKIE #2 *(handing him a cupcake that hums softly)*
You remembered you're already the party.

Jeff stands still, overwhelmed. Not in fear — in joy.

JEFF
I thought I was still figuring it out...

GRIZ
You are.
And you're also living it.
That's how this works.

The lights dim. Everyone gathers. A toast begins, led by the Council of All That's You.

COUNCIL (in unison)
To the one who laughed through his own awakening.
To the one who hugged his shadow.
To the one who didn't run when he saw his Self.

A single candle lights itself on the cosmic cupcake. Jeff looks around.

No test. No trick.
Just truth — and snacks.

JEFF *(quietly)*
You mean I'm home?

VOICE FROM EVERYWHERE
You've always been.
We just threw this party so you'd notice.

[END SCRIPTLET]

21

Jeff Forgets Everything

... and It's Perfect.
"And there was tea."
No thoughts. Just vibes.

Scene:
Morning. Early light filters through the window. Jeff wakes slowly — no visions, no downloads, no urgent cosmic tasks.

He sits up, blinks, and realizes...

He doesn't remember anything.
No glyphs. No ego maps. Not even his cosmic grocery list.

Just breath.

JEFF (*softly*)
Huh.

He walks to the kitchen. The kettle sings, not like a prophecy, but like it's just happy to be hot. He pours tea.

No meaning.
No message.

Just steam rising.

He sits at the table and watches the light crawl across it.
No internal monologue.
No impulse to post about it.

He smiles.

A knock at the door.
It's a neighbor he doesn't recognize.
They smile too. No reason. Just shared existence.

NEIGHBOR
Beautiful day.

JEFF
I have no idea what day it is.

NEIGHBOR
Even better.

They part ways. Jeff sits again. Forgets what he was thinking. Doesn't mind.

Outside, a bird sings the most ordinary song imaginable.
It moves him to tears.

He doesn't know why.
Which is exactly why it works.

No signposts.
No assignment.
Just this.

He takes a sip of tea and laughs — low, long, and real.

JEFF
I don't remember who I'm supposed to be...
But I love who I am.

And with that?

The scene fades.
The page turns.
The Manual closes — for now.

[END SCRIPTLET]

22

Epilogue

Returning Home.
He was never really lost.

Scene:

Interior — soft light. Not quite a spaceship. Not quite a body. Walls pulse with memory. The floor is made of language that forgot it was sacred. Jeff floats, weightless, not in space, but in himself.

He touches a wall — it shimmers and forms around his hand.

JEFF
(quietly)
I thought home was somewhere I had to go.

A low hum responds. Not a voice. A knowing.

VESSEL
You never left.

JEFF
But I walked through lives and lifetimes. I built temples. I searched the stars.

VESSEL
You built bodies. Each one was a chapter.
Each step forward was a spiral inward.

JEFF
So... you're not my ship?

VESSEL
I'm your form. Your rhythm. Your reminder.
I'm what happens when the Infinite chooses to *walk*.

JEFF
(amazed)
I painted this. Years ago. I didn't understand what I was remembering.

VESSEL
You did. You just hadn't caught up to your own echo yet.

Jeff places a hand on his chest. The same patterns glow faintly there — rivers, contours, galaxies curled into sinew.

JEFF
I'm the vessel.
I'm the terrain.
I'm the home I thought I'd lost.

Silence — not empty, but full. Full of the One breathing through form. Full of presence. Full of return.

In the background, a single blue orb pulses in rhythm with his heartbeat. The words appear on the wall:

"WELCOME HOME."

[END SCRIPTLET]

Apendix

THE MINI PISKIE PHRASEBOOK:

SPEAK LIKE A PISKIE IN 7 LAUGHS OR LESS

General Rule of Piskie:

- There are no tenses. Only **vibes**.
- Grammar? Please. We're flying.
- Laughter is both **verb** and **currency**.
- The same sound can mean three things depending on eyebrow angle.

Essential Piskie Phrases

1. "Tee-ha-ha!"
Meaning:

- "I see your soul."
- "That thought was silly, please let it go."
- Or: "You stepped on sacred moss, but we forgive you."

2. "Flim-flicka-BOOP."
Said while twirling in place.
Meaning:

- "Let's try that again, but with 70% more joy."

3. "Mmmmhm-hmm!" *(with eyebrows raised)*
Meaning:

- "Yes, and..."
- "You're close."
- "You just passed an inner test you didn't know you were taking."

4. "Twinkle-snort."
Meaning:

- "Accidental enlightenment. Well done."

5. "Glee to your tree!"
Standard greeting. Roughly translates to:

- "I bless your roots, branches, weirdness, and shoes."

6. [Silence, followed by a wink]
Meaning:

- "I know what you mean."

- "Let's not say it out loud. It'll dissolve the magic."
- "I love you."

7. "Zhhhht!" *(sharp exhale while tapping your heart)*
Meaning:

- "Truth just landed."
- "Stay there. Don't run. This is real."

Cultural Notes:

- If a Piskie hands you a rock, it's either a blessing, a question, or their life story. Don't throw it.
- "Being serious" in Piskie culture is seen as a temporary flu. They'll wrap you in giggles until it passes.
- No one *owns* language. It's shared like snacks.

Closing Phrase:

"Light to your left shoe, and freedom to your giggle."
Use this when parting ways with a fellow traveler who remembered a little more today.

Fin

ALL THIS AND MORE...

Scene:
A nondescript café at the edge of everywhere. Slightly too quiet. Slightly too real. Jeff is stirring honey into his tea, watching the steam rise like it might spell something out.

He's alone at his table — or thinks he is.

VOICE (gentle, direct, and somehow familiar)
You're waiting for permission again, aren't you?

Jeff looks up. Across the table: a man in dusty sandals and soft eyes. Could be a traveler. Could be... more.

JEFF
Depends who's asking.

TRAVELER
You are.
(pause)
You've always been the one asking. And the one answering.

JEFF
(squints)
You're not really... Him, are you?

TRAVELER
Does it matter?

Jeff laughs nervously.

JEFF
No, I guess not.
But if you were... could you remind me again? That part — the part about what comes next?

The Traveler smiles. Not with superiority — with recognition.

TRAVELER
"All this... and more you will do."

JEFF
(chokes slightly on his tea)
Wait — you were serious?

TRAVELER
Always. But seriousness isn't required.

JEFF
So... it wasn't just metaphor?

TRAVELER
Metaphor is reality with the mask off.
You think miracles are rare because you forgot you're made of them.

JEFF
Okay, but — like — healing, walking on water, radical love?
I'm just Jeff.

TRAVELER
So was I.

Beat. Silence folds around them. Jeff stares into his cup, which suddenly overflows — not with tea, but with light.

TRAVELER (softly)
You're not here to worship what I did.
You're here to **remember what you are.**

JEFF
And what's that?

TRAVELER
The One. With legs. And doubt. And power you haven't even named yet.

Jeff looks out the café window. The world seems... softer. Truer. A bird lands, sings something that sounds suspiciously like "Get on with it."

He turns back.

The Traveler is gone.

But on the table, written in spilled honey:

"All this and more, Jeff. You already are."

[END SCRIPTLET]

www.ingramcontent.com/pod-product-compliance
Lightning Source LLC
Chambersburg PA
CBHW071214120626
46546CB00006B/2552